Our Only Time Is Now

Clues for Dealing with Spiritual Challenges

By Milena

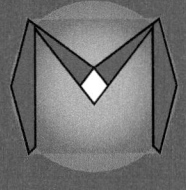

M PUBLISHING

CONTENTS

OUR ONLY TIME IS NOW 4
ETERNAL CHANGING 10
ENDNOTES 27
BIBLIOGRAPHY 29

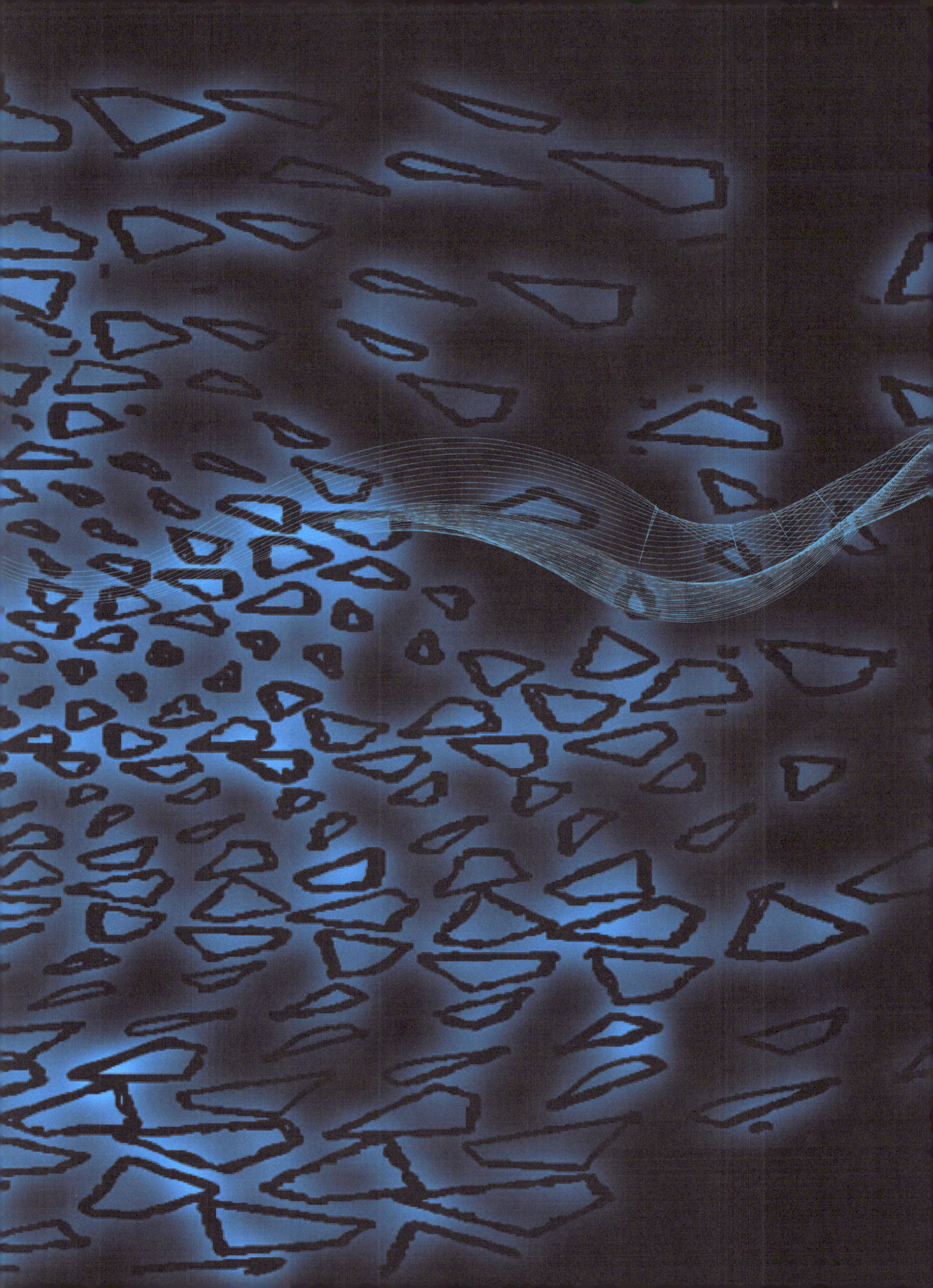

OUR ONLY TIME IS NOW

EVOLUTION ON EARTH	5
RESURRECTION	6
OUR THOUGHTS ARE MORE REAL AND POWERFUL THAN OUR PHYSICAL BODY	8
REMEMBERING SELF	10
SACRED GEOMETRY	13
NOW IS FOREVER	15

EVOLUTION ON EARTH

Fate and times revolve, days pass and the one who completes his/her cycle falls again on earth like a comet. The Heavens are Lights and Divine Lights. Provided You can bear their Power, You can always be Present. Otherwise, You can not recognise Yourselves. You live in Your World with a Veiled Awareness, You remain in nonexistence.

The Knowledge Book
(F24, p 378, par 8)[1-1]

OUR LIFE ON EARTH IS A KIND OF SCHOOL

Planet Earth is currently in an evolutionary dimension where energy is dense and manifested in the physical form of crude matter. Our life on it is a kind of school with a learning environment set up by the Creator, the Celestial Hierarchy and Mother Earth. Having agreed on the beauties and challenges of this unique cosmic classroom, each one of us on a personal level elucidates the reasons for being here. The awareness and consciousness that we gain, guide us towards the realisation of our predetermined objectives for the given lifetime.

1.1 – The Dimension of Truth is a totality supervised by the All-Truthful[1-3]

How big is God?
Big enough to have created the Universe... yet small enough to know your name small enough to be here today small enough to be next to you as you read these words.

Kryon[1-5]
through Lee Carroll

EVOLUTION

Energy has been brought into existence by a power unknown to us. Energy is subject to evolvement and for the purpose of assessing it, the energy dimensions are recognised[1-2]. The energies of human beings have always been enabling our integration with the higher dimensions.

All information is present in the human being, as truths have been coded into our genes to be used when we are ready. Access to them depends on the level of consciousness of a person. The unveiling and utilization of our genetic potential is, therefore, the reason why the human factor is exposed to educational and evolutionary influences.

Evolution is a process of progress into the next higher dimension. The aim is for the evolving energies of our biological body to gather on the same coordinate, and to integrate with their essence connected to the *Spiritual plan*. Thus we evolve to reach perfection which comes when we match our potential on the material plan with our potential on the *Spiritual plan*. Evolution is needed for the development of our cellular potential, our thought and our consciousness[1-4].

Evolvement is a law for everything that has been brought into existence.
Metamorphosis is eternal.
Consciousness evolves towards the infinite consciousness.

The hour strikes in the evolution of every planet and its humanity when they must express the full peace, harmony, Perfection and the Divine Plan of the system to which they belong. When that hour strikes, humanity either moves forward and fulfils that plan, or whatever portion will not come into alignment with the new Activity removes itself to another school room of the Universe, until those personalities learn obedience to life.

Saint Germain[1-6]

RESURRECTION

TOGETHER ON THIS FLYING SAUCER CALLED PLANET EARTH

As consciousnesses, epitomised in a human form and eager to acquire needed experiences, we have inhabited this living flying saucer called Planet Earth where, inevitably and purposefully, we have been exposed to orchestrated cosmic influences. The age in which we live is characterised by exceptional dynamism of changes, and the integration of genuine human beings throughout the universe. The greatness of that evolutionary task makes our time highly demanding.

The inter-dimensional shift that planet Earth is currently going through in her own evolution, requires from all its dwellers to make the same shift in order to follow her and her cosmic destiny. For that reason, all beings on the planet are undergoing specific and rapid changes on a cellular level. According to the *divine plan*, the changes are induced by special cosmic currents which have been sent to the planet since the beginning of the 20th century. These currents deliver necessary information, as cosmic pores, to all life forms on Earth and help earthly bodies to transform and prepare for existence in more advanced dimensions.

I am the resurrection and the life. He who believes in me will live, even though he dies.

The Bible
(John 11:25,26)

EXPANDING AWARENESS FROM TERRESTRIAL TO COSMIC

We live in an age of resurrection, heralded in religious books given to our planet as a mass consciousness training programme from the Cosmos. What resurrects is our essence, our awareness and our consciousness. We wake up by understanding truth beyond religious dimension and, at the same time, expand our attention from the domain of the terrestrial to the domain of the universal/cosmic.

Highly stimulated by special cosmic influences, resurrection is a process of activating our latent brain codes on our way to higher frequencies and supreme realities. The characteristic of this period is reverse proportionality, which means that truth is just the opposite of what we have been conditioned to believe.

Resurrection is also a time of rapid knowledge attainment and of great technological advancement. Surrounded by material abundance, the human being is challenged to shift its attention from the physical to the metaphysical, from the visible to the invisible. The search for the eternal truths, while seeking spiritual self-realisation, speeds up our resurrection.

Consciousness is geometric-conveyed patterns of energy. – Dr Noel Huntley[1-7]

EVERYTHING CREATED IS EQUALLY IMPORTANT

On the path of resurrection we are also maturing in our relationship with Mother Earth. We are becoming aware of her sentient being, busy on her evolutionary path yet committed to taking care of her children.

However, under the lights of the heavens, Earth is not only our current life stage but that of numerous other co-travellers like ants, birds and trees. The thought that everything created is equally important, be it on Earth or throughout the entire Creation, is becoming more familiar to us with each new day.

▲ *1.2 – The bigger picture and universal truth are available in proportion to our readiness for them*

All That Is is like a huge cosmic soup in which the ingredients influence one another while producing the final taste. Everything is interconnected, though the threads are still invisible to us.

▼ *1.3 – By illustrating the principle of fractals, Russian dolls remind us that there is always a new, bigger version of ourselves*

THERE IS ALWAYS A BIGGER PICTURE

There is always a bigger picture of reality than the one exposed to our immediate perception and available to our comprehension. Thus, one of the purposes of religious books is to teach us to accept everything unconditionally, even when we are hurt or do not understand the reason of our experiences. This acceptance comes with the wisdom gained after many events lived through the chain of incarnations and with an unshakable faith in the positive intentions of the Creator and His *divine plan* reflected on our level each moment.

According to the absolute perfection of the Creation, each of our experiences is ultimately for our highest good and does appear in harmony and the order of *All That Is*. Adopting that view leads us to our inner peace.

OUR THOUGHTS ARE MORE REAL AND POWERFUL THAN OUR PHYSICAL BODY

CONSCIOUS CREATORS

We, the human beings on this planet, are currently receiving abundant cosmic support directed towards activating our latent divine attributes, and hence our accelerated evolution is proceeding silently but profoundly. Our discovery of the self and the essence-self is equally our discovery of the heavens, universes and our position in the ordinance of the Total. However, in order to reach that godly self we are to master our thought-forms and to learn how to use the energy and power we are entrusted with.

Since the universal truths which are our biological legacy are inherent in us, it is time to consciously claim them. By surrendering to our inner knowing and guidance, we harmonise with these truths and get to know ourselves better. We will gradually rise to the level of the conscious creators of our reality, as those who trust in their own godly potential the Creator gave to us in the moment of our first conception. What we call synchronicities and miracles will then become a regular phenomenon in our life and we will consider our thoughts more real and powerful than our physical body.

THERE IS NO FORCING IN ANYTHING

On this path, it is necessary to understand the role of dualism in us and around us, and therefore to illuminate our dark side. Dualism is going to be experienced for as long as the lessons it holds for us are not learnt, for as long as we do not understand that we are all an indivisible ONE that experiences itself through innumerable self-aspects.

The future world is being shaped in the NOW. On the way to the happy tomorrows and brotherly-sisterly union of all, unconditional love – tolerance – patience – self-sacrificing – humbleness – goodwill, are imperative. Consciously lived, these qualities have the power to reinforce even the potential of our universe. Choosing to practise them is a matter of our personal spiritual maturity.

On the divine path there is no forcing in anything. Each one of us is a free Spirit, with a free will. However, our free will is narrowed to the energy and evolutionary medium of our planet and to our actual consciousness level.

The finest fruits of our free will come when, by exercising it, we rely on our conscience and common sense.

> Thought is a vehicle of transmission of unknown energy beyond matter. The *Technological dimension* keeps record of all our thoughts, in each breath we take, and stores them in the cosmic archives. It also automatically sends answers to our thought chains[1-8]. Only about 1/4 of our thoughts, however, are generated this way while up to 3/4 are a mere reflections of someone else's thoughts on us. Since we cannot know the origin of our thoughts, we should not believe each and every one of them that enter our mind but should rather reflect upon them.

MASTERING THE USE OF ENERGY

Thoughts and emotions are energy. Words are energy. Being is an energy process. All these energies constantly emanate from people on this planet and their quality determines our future. Similar energies are grouped and empowered. From those unified fields, they return as events which we experience. So, our thoughts, our emotions, our words are prescriptions in the form of patterns. They influence the geometry of the ever fluctuating energy matrix and condition the manifestation that follows. It is therefore immensely important to understand and perfect the use of our energy, and to find the highest purpose for it.

We are each a consciousness that needs to monitor its own energy and to develop self-discipline in positive thinking, affirmative speaking and acting. Gaining mastery over our energy will equip us with the ability to shape our reality so that we can initiate and maintain harmony within and without. However, a lasting peace, abundance and happiness, both individual and collective, can only be achieved through unity of our heart and our mind.

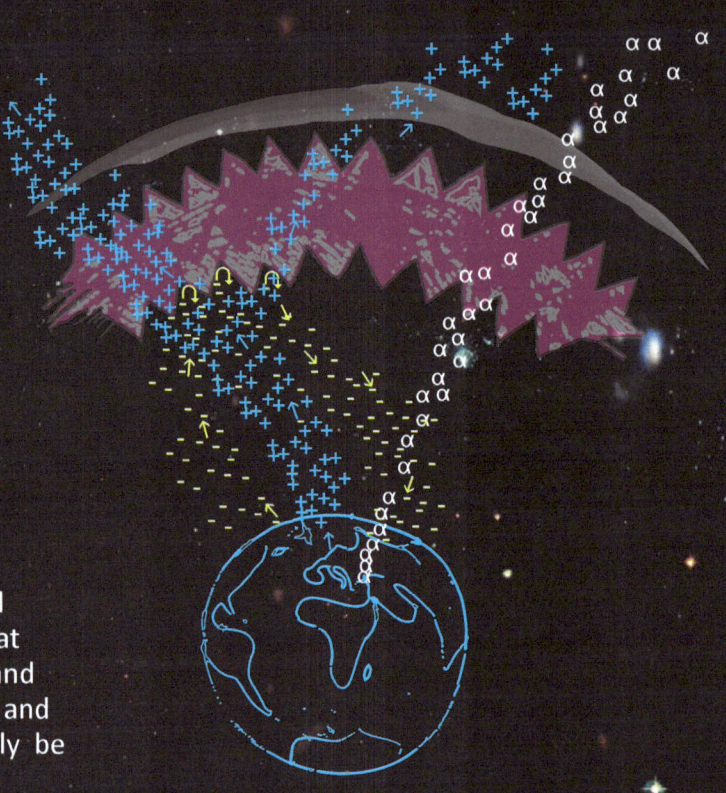

NOTHING HAPPENS BY CHANCE

Our words, our thoughts, our actions, affect not only us and those around us but faraway worlds and universes. No word or thought stays where it was conceived. As a geometrically patterned sound, or a thought-form, it is projected towards universal storages of either positive or negative energy, depending on its quality. From there, our thought energy is used for making new beings, worlds and universes. Great recycling is perpetually happening. Nothing in Creation is ever lost, purposeless, the same or alone. Everything brought into existence serves in the direction of its highest purpose and is part of the perfect equilibrium of eternal singularity.

If we can accept this premise, we can understand that within the everlasting oneness nothing ever happens by chance. For example, the fact that you are reading these lines right now is the result of pre-arranged circumstances that the parties involved have brought themselves into by making continuous choices at all times. Had anything been different, most likely, we would not be meeting now. Since we are, there is a reason for it. Maybe it is not a clear one yet, but this does not diminish its reality. Throughout the kingdom of the Creator, there is no such a thing as wasted time or wasted effort.

That which may look like chance is just a wider-scope probability that we draw to ourselves as a result of our thoughts and our decisions, combined with those of others. When what we call synchronicity occurs, the field of endless possibilities attracts our attention in order to teach us something. The bigger 'the chance', the more powerful the test and the message life holds for us.

In the endless tapestry of Creation, patterns hold its substance. So, no event will ever be without a pattern. Whether we recognise it or not, is irrelevant.

REMEMBERING SELF

OUR BEING BORN IS NOT A COINCIDENCE

We are ideas in the mind of God. While wearing this garment of the physical body, at times we walk away from Him into needed adventures of the tangible world in which we easily forget who we are, where we come from and where we are to go. However, despite our spiritual amnesia in the realm of matter, we are never left without God's supervising presence. His love and His programmes lead us into all experiences in the first place.

Recognising the God within is a process of evolving our consciousness to be respectful of the laws of our essence-energies which were sent into the existential dimension. Our being born is not a coincidence since, in the perfection of the Creation, randomness does not exist.

All is created with a cause born of a purpose and is innately capable of fulfilling its own mission within the *divine plan*.

LEARNING FROM LIMITATIONS

Human beings on this planet live their lives stretched between the heavens and Earth, Spirit and matter, epitomising their union. Throughout our life, we spiritualise matter and materialise the Spirit. While we heal the separation between earthly and celestial realms, we gradually evolve into higher forms of ourselves.

Despite all restrictions imposed on us, within the pronounced play of dark and light here in our temporary habitat on Earth, we ourselves have chosen to come because of the experiences we can have. One of them is to understand *duality consciousness* and to recognise the need to transcend it. Gaining such awareness is a necessary base for *unity consciousness*.

▲ *1.4 – Seemingly random, the local environment harmoniously fits into a bigger picture – illustration by Sándor Kabai*[1-9]

On that path, we have just started to see through many inherited veils of illusions related to what we consider to be real. At the moment, in Earth's school, we are learning how our perceptions and expectations hugely shape our experiences and how focusing on possibilities, rather than restrictions, is the key to conscious creating. Here, all lessons take place in a medium of godly and spiritual energies. They purify, train and strengthen us, helping us to reach our godly essence thus terminating our long-lasting state of self-alienation.

MEMENTO ^(I-10)

You shall remember Me, that I may remember you, and be thankful to Me; do not be unappreciative!^(I-11)

The Quran (2:152)

فَاذْكُرُونِي أَذْكُرْكُمْ وَاشْكُرُوا لِي وَلَا تَكْفُرُونِ

To find the meaning of our life, and therefore its purpose, is to discover our personal yet divine life mission. It requires a developed awareness of the Total and understanding of what/who we are within *All That Is*. Such an achievement runs parallel to the opening and evolving of our essence which best echoes the God Creator in us. His focal point within the human being is a divine cell placed into our heart. Its growing light is ready to show us the way Home, the way of transcending all separations.

This book is an encouragement in that direction. It reveals the eternal vocabulary of Creation and invites us to see the Creator, literally, in everything – for, truly, all has been created from His love translated into inter-related states of being and shapes that forever unfold according to his Divine Laws and Plans.

The gradually acquired capacity to recognise the Creator's immaculate self-organisation through geometric patterns helps us to align our being with those subtle creative forces that are pure, perfect and eternal. The energy that flows through them comes from the Source to refresh and feed us.

PATTERNS TEACH US ABOUT THE PURPOSE OF THINGS

Seeing beyond appearances and being able to recognise a constant behind the change, or patterns through which outer and inner worlds operate, is a measure of evolvement as an attribute of an experienced mind and expanded viewpoint. Patterns in nature are easier to notice than regularities in our relationships with other people or in our emotions.

We will keep repeating some experiences until eventually we see the rules and the patterns they follow. Patterns teach us about the purpose of things. Once we can distinguish them, we can spare ourselves from some experiences, particularly those that are not pleasant despite being ultimately didactical. Thus our liberation from being 'victims' of some situations is connected to our ability to recognise our personal behavioural patterns. Upon noticing them and understanding their purpose in relation to our highest good, we have an opportunity to transcend those aspects of our personality that have become conditioned, predictable and rigid.

Each pattern acknowledged means the expanding of our self-awareness. We therefore grow by noticing God's geometry in operation inside and outside of us. We also grow by learning to perceive spiritual principles behind all Creation and events. Once we understand the necessity and beauty of uncertainties (pattern arrangements of infinite potential), it would mean we have understood the role played by the intangible part of reality. When we discover the real power of our intent, it would mean we are ready to claim our divine legacy.

Liberation of the earthly-bound mind and orthodoxy is marked by the growing of the consciousness of human unity, expressed through social endeavours for the progress and betterment of all. Getting together in respect and love is crucial for the realisation of the final *Lordly order* on Earth called the *golden age*, the foundation of which is being laid at the moment.

SPIRALLING BACK TO ETERNAL SELF

We are godly seeds that have been nourished purposefully and patiently. Over the millennia, the *divine plan* made numerous efforts to introduce us to ourselves and to make us realise our godly essence. Returning to our eternal self is our cosmic destiny intended by the love of the one who has created us.

The geometry of God's love is the path and the way.
The light of God's love is everywhere and forever.

Like spirals, we are endlessly evolving and opening up to the beauty and might of God – heading towards our eternal self.

HARMONIC ECONOMY

Omnipresent-omniscient-neutral-natural consciousness is a totality. As such, it is single, yet it appears as a plurality of seemingly endless self-aspects organised through harmonic economy. By cascading via geometrical systems of reflection, omnipotent Totality of Consciousness propagates itself throughout the Creation.

SACRED GEOMETRY

WHAT IS SACRED GEOMETRY

There are many ways to describe *sacred geometry* and the benefits derived from using it. It is:

* a divine tool of Creation;

* a description of the very first movement of the mysterious One and of the ways this One has transformed into Two and into further plurality;

* a skeleton of shape and matter – an invisible energy pattern defined by numbers;

* a bridge between the unseen world and the world of visible form, as well as the path of energy/information/life force reflection through all levels of the Total;

* a revelation of the underlying unity of all Creation and the truth of infinite interconnections within the Total.

* a vibrational signature ingrained in all that has ever been created, and by becoming aware of it and studying it we gain a greater understanding of life and of ourselves.

EVERYTHING BELONGS TO ONE

THE LAW OF ONE
(prayer)

We are all ONE.
When one is harmed,
all are harmed.
When one is helped, all
are helped.
Therefore, in the name
of my being,
of who I AM,
and I am one with All
There Is,
I ask only for what is
the highest good
of all concerned
to happen.
I give thanks that
this is done.

Within the apparent disorder of *All That Is* lies an immaculate mathematical relationship between elements. Through a process of self-reflection, primordial singularity manifests its further self-aspects, as dimensions and universes of power, all the way to the skeins of the existential dimensions – all based on geometric patterns. These patterns are equally a skeleton of light, sound, colour and matter. Even phenomena like our emotions and awareness are ordered by the same principles of geometry, leaving no ground for chance. Nothing is exempt from the law of One.

◂ *1.5 – Our awareness and our consciousness have the same capacity, and it is infinite*

GUIDE TO THE CENTRE OF INNER STILLNESS

Sacred geometry provides us with a contextual understanding of Creation as an endless order and pure beauty. It stretches our awareness from the realm of matter to the realm of Spirit, where everything starts from, where we belong and where the truth is. Experience of *sacred geometry* triggers our sacredness by exciting the particle of the Creator within us. It is one of the ways of connecting with Him which can guide us to the centre of inner stillness. In order to stay there, we need to learn to harmonise all of our movements.

Let go and let God.
Do you understand?

It's giving up your power,
to be in the power of Being.

Flo Aeveia Magdalena[1-12]
(Sunlight on the Water)

Infinite movements converged into perfect stillness is a property of the so-called *zero point*. The *zero point* solves duality by balancing extreme states and transforms multiplicity into oneness. It is a physical definition of orgasm: immeasurable energy pulsating and being still at the same time.

◄ 1.6 – Focusing – a process that leads the waves towards their harmonic convergence. Our efficiency is in direct proportion to our power of focus.

SELF REMEMBERING SELF

Sacred geometry is an intangible template of our inner world.

Throughout the vastness of Creation, every geometrical pattern is connected to the preceding one. Using that network, self becomes aware of self by referencing towards the Source as the ultimate self-truth.

▼ 1.7 – Self that remembers self, resides in the geometric patterns of the life-force – illustration by Sándor Kabai

TOOL FOR EDUCATION OF THE SOUL

Human beings have been aware of *sacred geometry* since ancient times. It was taught in ancient mystery schools which considered *sacred geometry* an important tool in the education of the soul. Later these teachings were lost and nowadays we are returning to the old esoteric doctrine of non-separation. Modern scientists have gone beyond explaining only the structural side of matter and physical occurrences through it. **Daniel Winter**[I-13], for example, offers a refreshingly new understanding of how principles of *sacred geometry* work in our lives, like in the matters of love, compassion, self-awareness, bliss and addiction, or phenomena such as implosion, gravity, matter, mass, and even death. He sees the very nature of the life-force through it. Such findings offer reassurance whereby even the invisible aspects of life are based on tangible principles, and that we are living in an age in which sacredness, as a property of life, is becoming scientifically explainable.

▲ *1.8 – Linear perception recognises the beginning and the end, as two poles in between which our being/doing takes place*

▲ *1.9 – Each one of us is on the one-way walk which loops back into itself, into its own beginning*

ENDLESS WALK

… … … … Linear time is disappearing. What you perceive as time passing faster and faster is the effect of the higher energy planes in which you are living now, where everything is accelerating as Earth makes her way into the continuum – or, more accurately, as your consciousness grasps the actuality of that timelessness, the reality of eternity and infinity.

Matthew
through Suzanne
Ward[I-15]
(Matthew
Books)

Past and future are one a fabric, just like space. When we walk forward, we know that we leave some space behind but we are also aware that what is behind and what is ahead is actually one space. The same applies to time: the future and the past are one collection of potentials and happenings. Walking on a *Möbius strip*[I-14] illustrates this point. The line walked marks both sides – as one continuous surface of the strip (Fig. 1.10).

The way it is configured, the *Möbius strip* therefore does not divide space into inner and outer territories, which happens when a strip is made into a ring in the usual way without being twisted. Mere joining of the two ends of a long strip, after giving one end a 180-degree twist, creates an object which allows a new perception of its surrounding space and a new experiential dimension: at once two sides of the strip become one side and consequently what were the inner and outer territories of the ordinary ring become one boundless space. The *Möbius strip* is an example of two continuums merging. It convinces us that polarities can become indistinguishable if skilfully brought together.

The *Möbius strip*, which we can easily make from a piece of paper, also illustrates a phenomenon applicable to consciousness. The way we perceive polarities, the way we connect extremes into a meaningful whole, makes a big difference. From the material of our observation, we constantly choose whether we will make an ordinary ring or a twisted one like the *Möbius strip*. The choice is determined by the brain hemisphere our consciousness operates through in a given situation.

Left brain activity is responsible for linear thinking. It discerns dualism and creates the illusion of linear time. Lacking a holistic view, the left side is also not able to make a meaningful whole from polarised elements or within a non-logical context.

This side of the brain sees reality as a sum of the past, present and future. The higher reality is that there is only now, as an everlasting moment of existence, in which we continuously experience ourselves.

POWER POINT

Everything we ever experience makes an impact on our energy field. The results of our experiences are thus prime reasons for the experiences in the first place. What we consider as past is built into our substance on a cellular level and inevitably expresses itself through who we are now. Thus, there is no need to stay in the past as it is active in the now anyway. We are its current product being upgraded by every breath we take. Dwelling on the past is a futile waste of our energies in an often unconscious attempt to escape active participation in the now and the full encountering of our own self and God. For God lives in the eternal now where there is no past or future as all is happening simultaneously, at one time. Now is just another word for His mighty presence.

The future is unknown. To encounter the unknown is to encounter a new energy configuration and quality. Everything He has created, the God Creator can introduce to us by frequencies. Thus by getting used to new frequencies/energies, we are stepping deeper into the fibre of life, into our future. It is a process of simultaneous revealing of the secrets of Creation and of the power of our being. It is a path of our returning Home, to serve the Total, as the path of true re-membering.

1.10 – Möbius strip – a one-sided and one-edged surface. It forever folds in on itself.

Forever is composed of nows - Emily Dickinson

Dear Human Being, the duality wants you to believe that you are singular, living in a straight line, but that is not so. You're part of a group, and this group, like your life, is in a circle. This group is always with you.

Kryon
through
Lee Carrroll

Accepting the Will of God that is the energies/events He has prepared for us, knowing our real evolutionary needs more than we do, is certainly a sign of genuine faith and correct memory.

Now is the power point of existence, the best choice for investing our attention and inspiration. It is the single real aspect of time – the others are just a mind construct as its reference points.

Our only time is now. When we discover that now is forever, time loses its meaning. Then, it stands still while our being flows. And, we become one with life.

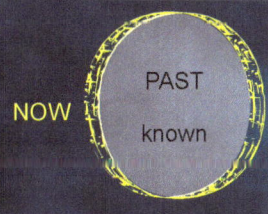

▲ 1.11 – The past is like the future – a picture gallery in our mind. The only difference is that mental pictures for the future are yet to be created, using our potential to intend, visualise and feel.

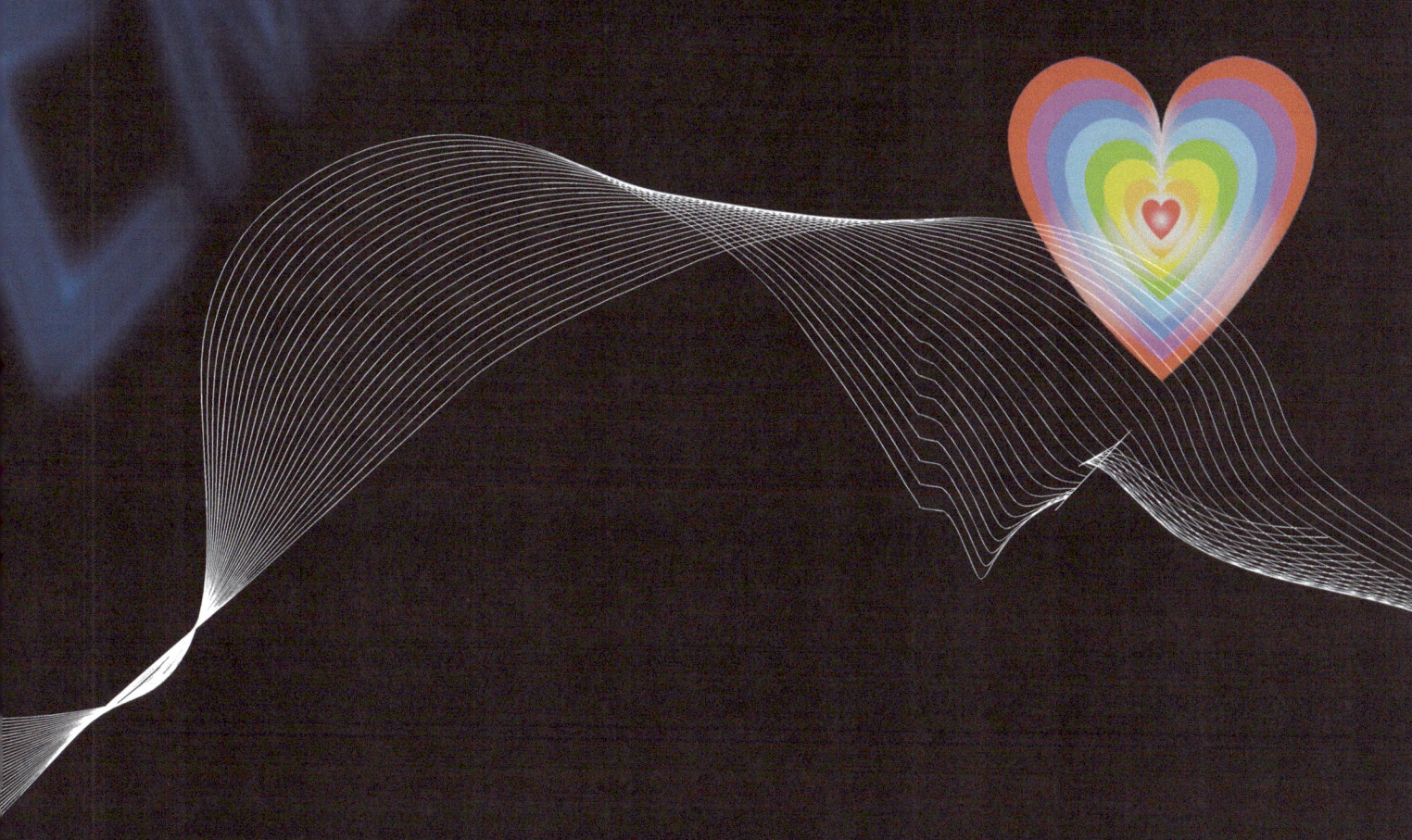

ETERNAL CHANGING

WE ARE ALWAYS SOMETHING NEW	19
DEMAND OF OUR TIME	19
MERGING OF MATTER AND SPIRIT	20
INVESTING IN OUR OWN FUTURE	21
PROGRAMMED EXPERIENCES	21
THROUGH TIME TILL TIMELESSNESS	22
THE LORD'S INTENTION	23
EXITING THE PROGRAMME OF DEATH	24
DIVINE ONENESS	24

2.1 – Wheel, the symbol of everlasting flow

However, it is not ever possible for You, in Your present states, to understand completely what I Am and what I Am not. Information given to You is for assisting Your Evolution and for Raising Your Cerebral Powers.

Great Power, The Knowledge Book (F 40, p 674, par 4)

WE ARE ALWAYS SOMETHING NEW

The purpose of all information given to our planet is for the human being to get used to the energy behind it. Information is therefore one of the ways we gradually adapt ourselves to new energies and get prepared for new dimensions, new worlds.

Due to our current evolutionary needs, over the last few decades more information has become available to our planet than in the last few millennia. However, no information has ever been disclosed to us until its time has arrived.

To form knowledge from the information requires grasping it beyond its verbal meaning. It requires being able to act from their energy coordinates in the manner of harmony, unity and the goodness for all. That way, the ultimate purpose of received information is fulfilled and we determine the level of its significance to the world of our personal truths.

The truth acquired through experience has the potential to make a shift in our consciousness. Hence all events we go through have one reason and that is to introduce us to our self, leading us towards our essence- GOD-consciousness, or godly self. In that process, we mature and are always something new. The evolvement of our personality, rather than its remaining the same, is therefore a valuable sign of our evolution.

Only a consciousness capable of continuously growing, parallel to the energies/information of the actual time, is a candidate for a lasting happiness.

DEMAND OF OUR TIME

ETERNAL CHANGING

An important aspect of our evolution is carried out through our mental efforts. The aim is for our brain to attract energies of unknown higher dimensions and make them available to our entire body, where our cells use them as a fuel for life's potential. An active brain gradually enlarges its capacity to reach more intense cosmic energy layers (information) and in that way strengthens our biological constitution.

Every shift in consciousness leads to a special moment when a society begins to better understand her relationship to the Divine.

Galactic Federation of Light through Sheldan Nidle[II-1]

The Cosmos does not support separatisms and antagonisms on our planet. On the contrary, following the direct command of the Lord, special cosmic currents, which have been showering our planet since the year 1900, have caused fundamental changes on all levels of life and have stimulated manifestation of a more positive reality in a faster way. Under the influence of these currents, and according to the level of personal consciousness, we encounter events that grind an unrefined consciousness and help advance the one that is able to grow. However, it is not the Cosmos that does this selection. The Cosmos only sends the influences which create the necessary medium for the strengthening of our cellular potential and for getting it ready to deal with the energies of the universal dimension. But, each one of us chooses our own response to these divine evolutionary triggers. In other words, we are personally responsible for our own survival, evolvement and happiness.

Since human beings on our planet are granted free will, it is not planned for us to be manipulated from a distance, as in the case of robots; neither is it possible that the positive results in our development can be achieved by force. That is why after the 6000 years during the three *orders of the Lord*, each one of them lasting 2000 years, when humanity was left to evolve through the godly doctrines of the sacred books, the majority of human beings failed to grasp the real meaning and reasons behind these books and the cosmic energies, as well as to understand the purpose of the events they had gone through – therefore have not achieved the desired evolutionary level. According to the objectives of the *Lordly orders*, it has been expected that, at the end of this long training period, by the year 2000, an average consciousness level on our planet would be able to attract and assimilate the energy of the 18th evolutionary dimension (*KU* frequency – the 72nd energy dimension) [II-2]. That evolutionary state, of saturation with the *alpha* energies, is so-called *religious fulfilment* and is a precondition for stepping onto the universal path of evolvement through the *beta* energies of the 19th evolutionary dimension (*Omega dimension* = the 76th energy dimension). In other words, until an individual completes the evolution through the *alpha* programme of the *religious dimension*, he/she cannot open the programme containing the *beta* energies of the *universal dimension*.

MERGING OF MATTER AND SPIRIT

Alpha energies are godly energies, from the syllabus of religious education offered through sacred books, represented in virtues like love, faith and unconditional acceptance, while *beta energies* are the spiritual energies of wisdom, responsibility, intellect and essence-consciousness. Individuals who remain on the *alpha* energy level are not able to fully utilise their faculty of logic. After entering through crown chakra, *alpha* purifying energies do not stay in our body but pass through it. On the other hand, the *beta* energies that we have attracted to ourselves are partly reflected onto our surroundings and partly stored in our bone cells[II-3].

A human being who is not able to attract special cosmic currents carrying *beta* energies that regenerate and strengthen our cellular constitution, is in the state of self-annihilation. It is destined to stay disconnected from its divinely entrusted spiritual power, living like a bird with one wing only. Cosmic energies stimulate the evolution of conscious energy towards the activation of the spiritual potential that belongs to its material form. They actually help in the merging of matter and Spirit, which is a process of strengthening enough of our materialised energy so that it can claim its essence-energy from the *Spiritual plan*[II-4]. The integration of body's energy with its own spiritual essence makes the body indestructible and qualifies it for eternity. That is exactly the path and the aim of the energy appearing as a *human being* – to attain the qualities necessary for permanently remaining in existence. Then, as super human residents of much higher energy dimensions, we would become the creators and supervisors of the new universes and the ordinances of the future.

INVESTING IN OUR OWN FUTURE

In the medium of the cosmic transformation prepared on our planet, in accordance with the *divine plan* of accelerated evolution, those who are not able to draw special cosmic energies cannot undergo necessary evolution and are doomed to remain at the terrestrial level of consciousness. *Terrestrial consciousness* is caught in the whirlpool of energies dominated by the ego and fear as well as religious and various terrestrial attachments like habits, passions and taboos. *Terrestrial consciousness* perpetuates chaos and negativities. Unless it transcends the attraction with the terrestrial, this consciousness will not be able to reach the divine waves and be transformed into *cosmic consciousness* to meet the demand of our time. In other words, if *terrestrial consciousness*, as a slave to its own terrestrial views, does not manage to grow beyond itself, it will not escape from depression and transcend the dimension of tests and evolution. Thus, due to its own low frequency, it will be unable to connect with the currents that are under the protecting supervision of the *divine plan*.

At the moment, an insufficient number of people attract special cosmic currents of a growing intensity that shower the Earth. Consequently, the distribution of these currents between humans and nature is disturbed and nature is affected by cosmic energies more than anticipated. Human beings who do not undergo the evolutionary transformation needed, are directly responsible both for their own situation and for that of the planet. Instead of witnessing more resurrections of consciousness, we are witnessing more frequent natural catastrophes.

In the medium of a comfortable life, the human being unwillingly changes, which slows down his/her own evolution. For that reason, our sufferings, shocks and distress are an unavoidable way of releasing the lower aspects of our own personalities, of completing karma, of achieving saturation with *alpha* energies and with *all terrestrial* – in order for the *terrestrial consciousness* to transform into *cosmic consciousness* in the shortest possible time. All our life experiences are an investment in our future. Therefore, not only is it meaningless to complain about the difficulties in our path, it will also make things worse by bringing the negative energy in. Instead, an unconditional acceptance of everything that comes our way and conscious inner work will get us closer to the evolution of the *Omega dimension*. Our self, others, planet Earth and the entire universe will benefit from our attracting and reflecting the energy of this dimension.

PROGRAMMED EXPERIENCES

While we are walking towards the light of the *dimension of truth*, towards our eternal self, it is paradoxical yet real that there are no good or bad choices. In order to understand this, we need to start from the premise that we cannot step onto the path of universal evolvement unless we let go of terrestrial wishes and passions. However, the only way to transcend these is to live them to the fullest. Our life is therefore like a series of computer programs, timed for entering into necessary experiences, both pleasant and unpleasant, and the kundalini energy inside us is charged with leading into these experiences[II-5]. This energy decodes deeply hidden needs of our physical body which are part of our so-called *destiny*, yet they can be unknown to us. Kundalini energy introduces our hidden needs to our awareness. Then, the intellect, as the commanding factor within the facets of awareness, if necessary, leads us into a state of obsession with the needs forced by this energy. According to the design of the Creator, we do not have control over kundalini. That energy is even independent of the law of cause and effect. Thus, it is not for us to form negative opinions about anyone's behaviour.

THROUGH TIME TILL TIMELESSNESS

Our evolvement has always been subject to the law of graduality which means that no progressive shift happens till we reach the necessary energy threshold. Following this law, billions of centuries have passed since, as a particle, we have embarked on the path towards becoming a human being. Starting from a micro energy that in seven stages evolved through inorganic material forms, we went through a further seven stages of living beings to reach the human form. Under the light of consciousness that has grown through seven additional stages, we are now about to merge with the macro consciousness of the Total[II-6].

According to that objective, in all 1800 *mini atomic wholes*, or *mini atomics*, within our *natural alpha Gürz*, where, as an offspring of the Adam-kind, lives Human-kind, human beings are exposed to programmes of evolution supervised by the *All-Dominating*. However, in our entire *Gürz*, there is only one *mini atomic* that is a medium of godly energy. It is the *mini atomic* in which our planet is to be found. Furthermore, our planet is its *nucleic world*. That means that our planet has served as the nucleus around which our *mini atomic* is formed through time processes. Our *mini atomic* is actually very special, because it was the first ever *mini atomic* that has appeared during the formation of our *natural alpha Gürz* and is the closest one to the *Second Universe*. All entities from the remaining 1799 *mini atomics* in our *natural Gürz* (from 1799x1800 = 1.439.200 universes)[II-7] are obliged to have their final evolutionary exams in our *mini atomic whole* and on our planet, since here is a school for gaining godly personality by educating consciousnesses on the godly path. Tests and lessons take place in our personal thought dimensions and reflect on our behaviour in circumstances continuously arranged to best suit our evolutionary needs. The objective is to achieve virtues such as: responsibility, humbleness, patience, tolerance, self-sacrifice, forgiveness, gratitude, conscience, unconditional love.

In order to graduate in this godly school of life, so far everyone has been given three incarnations within the 26000 years of the *Gürz crystal*'s natural cycle, and so through three cycles which makes it nine chances all together[II-7]. Since the programme of these cycles will terminate at the end of 22nd century, it is desirable for as many human beings of our *natural Gürz* as possible to complete their evolution through the godly doctrines (reach *KU* frequency – the 18th evolutionary dimension), then to enter into the evolution of the 19th evolutionary dimension (*Omega* – RAN planet) and succeed in it. From the 23rd century, such an opportunity will not be available anymore because, by then, the existing programme of evolution (*Alpha* entrance – *Omega* exit) will come to an end; due to the objectives of the *IV order of the Lord*, or the *golden age* period, which our planet started to participate in at the commencement of the year 2000. The word *Quran* is in fact a cipher, of this evolutionary path, placed in the very title of the last sacred book.

During the three *cosmic ages* that comprise the 20th, 21st and 22nd centuries, the foundation of the *golden age* is going to be laid while the speeded-up evolution and the final selection of the consciousnesses within our *natural Gürz crystal* is taking place (for the Cosmos, firstly we are consciousness and then a physical body!). In this three-centuries-long transition period between the *III* and *IV order of the Lord*, human beings are going through the *last judgement* and the *resurrection* so that the consciousnesses that have a future in more evolved realities can be selected. The first criterion is for them to reach *KU* frequency, by being incarnated in the medium of godly energy, and then to attract and to assimilate *beta* energy from *Omega*, the 19th evolutionary dimension. At one moment, on that evolvement path, our essence becomes our eye and our word. Upon grasping the truth beyond the *religious dimension*, we take part in the universal programmes of the *golden age* by serving other human beings and the Total.

When our thought is able to respond to the time energy of the world medium in which it operates and to utilise it, that is, when our brain potential gains more power by attracting ever higher energy/information from unknown universal dimensions, our thought is on its way to transcending itself, and its own speed. That is how it is going to pass from time to timelessness.

THE LORD'S INTENTION

Interestingly, in the programmes of the *golden age*, the peak of individual evolutionary achievement is manifested through serving others self-sacrificingly. It comes with the maturity of our heart that longs to express gratitude to the Creator for the gift of life and all His mercy. It is the level of mission-consciousness which will usher us into higher worlds since it gets under control the unconstructive behaviour of the ego and its need to prove itself. In mission-consciousness, the WHOLE is more important than individual. We surrender ourselves to it and reach self-realisation that way. It is a consciousness of UNITY in action, consciousness that has understood the function of opposites within the perfection of the Total. With its love and allegiance, it supports the Total and finds its own purpose in it.

The time of individualism and leaders belongs to the past. Now is the time to unite all religions and races of people into a consciousness that serves the Total, which has created us and maintains our life. The reflection of the physical and spiritual transformation from the level of the universe onto our planet, initiates this global tendency. The Cosmos has been meticulously preparing us for this evolutionary stage, by strengthening our genes for millennia. For that reason, extremely capable genes are present on the planet now. They can successfully deal with the fast tempo of changes and the strong energies coming from the open sky. As a part of a genetically coded programme, these cosmic energies activate mission-consciousness when a person achieves an evolvement level parallel to the energy of the time.

Our personal future entirely depends on the ability of our consciousness to grow, and therefore on the efforts of our evolving energy in that direction. The truths about it are now being disclosed to us in all clarity because, according to the universal laws, the time has come for that. By reaching the *KU* frequency, and by transcending the *religious consciousness*, we are exiting the programme of the sacred books and the periods of mysticism and are entering the age of truth based on the energies of the Universal dimension.

The only direct book of the LORD on our planet, that contains the universal energies of all nine layers of the 19th evolutionary dimension (Omega), is *The Knowledge Book*. Even though it is entirely an *Omega* book, *The Knowledge Book* is at the same time the book of endless dimensions. It was given as a gift to our planet at the end of 20th century. The book reflects on us the *beta* energies of the *Omega dimension* from a close distance and hence enables those who read it, study it or copy it in their handwriting, to absorb these high energies in the fastest and most efficient way. Since sacredness is an attribute related to the *alpha* programme of religious education, *The Knowledge Book*, carrying *beta* energies only, is not a sacred book even though it has arrived through the Lord's *Alpha channel* as have all sacred books. *The New Testament* has introduced to our planet the energy of the 9th evolutionary dimension and the *seven layers* of the *terrestrial knowledge*; *The Quran* – the energy of the 18th evolutionary dimension and the *seven layers of the celestial knowledge* while *The Knowledge Book* declares the truth from *the seven layers of the universal knowledge* by the use of the energy from the 19th evolutionary dimension.

Each one of us is a unique manifestation of the Lord's intention. According to that intention, for the first time ever, the entrance and the exit doors of the *Omega dimension* are opened to us. Beyond the *Omega* exit door, on Beta Nova, He is waiting for us[II-8] to prepare us directly for the next level of existence He has planned for us in His *beta* stage of creation.

The aim of the *IV order of the Lord* is the establishment of the *Atlanta golden dimension* anew, in the context of the Total, by creating a flower-like formation over the billions of centuries. The single nucleus of that flower will be obtained by loading onto our *natural alpha Gürz* the compressed potential of all artificial *alpha Gürzes*. Reinforced that way, during the time, our *natural alpha Gürz* will become the centre surrounded by six new *Beta Gürz crystals*[II-9] appearing as flower petals. Meanwhile, at some point, extremely strong *berzah*[II-10] energies will come into effect and annihilate all that does not contain *beta* spiritual energy. Our staying in existence therefore is directly dependant on the ability of our evolving energies to merge with their essence power present in the *Spiritual plan*. The most important function of *The Knowledge Book* which carries the *beta* energies, is in its offering the solution which removes fundamental apprehension about our future: Beta Nova[II-11] or *berzah* of non-existence.

EXITING THE PROGRAMME OF DEATH

In accordance with its own evolutionary needs and the programmes of the terrestrial school, the human being is tested by other human beings and these interactions expose our evolutionary deficiencies. Thus, we are, actually, an evolutionary mirror to one another. These mirrors reflect the true level of our evolvement in each of our encounters. The human being also needs other humans to be lit by their light. Human beings that reach the energies of the higher dimensions, by emanating them to their own surroundings, help those who are not capable of attracting these energies on their own. So, human communication is a prism which reflects our evolutionary processes.

Our path is from the inside to the outside: from self-awareness towards socialisation and from planetary integration towards the inter-planetary unification of particular consciousness levels. According to the accelerated programme of evolvement, on our way to exit *Omega* and our *natural Gürz*, in this lifetime we may reach the *Reality of the Unified Humanity* and get permission to go to *Beta Nova* – a nucleus world of the first *mini atomic whole* of the first out of six future *Beta Gürzes*. From all *alpha Gürzes*, those who successfully complete their evolutionary programmes will gather there. After aeons of evolution, the human being has reached the evolvement dimensions beyond religious energies. To attain this stage, every single step needed to be deserved according to the criteria of the *divine plan*. During the next 200 years, the human beings on our planet are going to be exposed to the final testing of the entire education through the energies of our *natural Gürz*. From the 23rd century, only those who manage to absorb the *beta* energies of *Omega dimension* in their bones will be able to incarnate on this planet, because Earth is going to become a medium of very powerful energies. With the unfolding of the *golden age*, by then, the programmes of reincarnation and death will come to an end.

DIVINE ONENESS

Arriving at the end of this book signifies the closing of the circle of one experience and, consequently, arriving at a new level of self as the starting point for a next circle. It may also look like an ending, or a point of separation. However, there is no separation except in our mind. The book once read, like any other experience, is an energy mark that stays in us with an intensity that suits our evolving energy.

Separation is a man-made concept which is lived at a particular level of evolution. In the same way as we have adopted it, it would be natural to grow out of it, by starting to consciously comply with the universal energies and laws.

(II-12)

The experiences we accumulate, more and more convincingly expose to us the subtle interconnectedness of thoughts, words and events. Everything in the entire Creation, alive and so-called non-alive, is purposefully together as a part of the same grandiose body of the eternal oneness. Like the cells of God's organism, though seemingly separate, we perform in harmony with and for the purpose of its systems, orders and ordinances.

According to the hierarchy of the *divine order*, to enter the universal chambers is possible only for the consciousness able to draw universal energies and gain awareness of the ordinance of the Total. Such a consciousness naturally and unconditionally begins to support the perfection of the Total, while gratefully serving it through correct thoughts, words and deeds. The human being not capable of supervising its own self is hence subjected to an evolution. Our current evolutionary education, within a necessary energy range, is additionally facilitated by special cosmic pores coming through the open sky to accelerate the lifting of the veils from our cerebral codes. As our genetic potential is more activated, we unmistakably recognise the calls, from the highly evolved worlds, for moving into a state of a more conscious belonging to the oneness.

The endless oneness was, is and will always be. We are each a spark of God's Consciousness and, from the unique personal coordinates of the life-matrix, experience that oneness while simultaneously creating both personal and collective reality. Now is the time to do it with an alert mind. Now is the time to reach conscious love with the Creator and life, so that we can start shining to the fullest. The glow of that sacred light that the Creator placed into our genetic code, He rightly expects from us. That is why now, faster than ever before, cosmic energies are stimulating our spiritual potentials, our dreams and visions; new paradigms and a new us.

Anachronously supporting old concepts, and holding onto old beliefs, would only continue to produce old results. The way to bring in the new is to go with the energy of the time, stay open and sharpen our spiritual focus. As we shift our attention to the desirable new, we deprive it of the old that we intend to transcend. Such an investment of our energy, contributes to the manifestation of desired reality.

Only the better we can build a better life of a brotherly and sisterly world of peace, love and harmony. In this process of eternal changes and noble intentions, if we are still bothered with some doubts it is a sign that we have not purified and matured enough on the godly path; having not accepted God's Will and understood law of cause and effect which leaves no place for accidental or purposeless events and experiences.

Scientific/spiritual explanations of the secrets of coming into existence, of the *Genesis* and functions of the highest powers of the Total, from the *dimension of truth* are nowadays offered to the human being who is searching about his/her own origin and purpose of existence. Answers to the questions of *who we are*, *where we come from* and *which paths are in front of us* are available and will be reached when we are ready for them; when our being can receive them in a harmonious way and make use of their energy.

I was Stone, I was Earth, I became a Blade of Grass, I became a Flower, I becam

COME, COME, COME

(II-13)

تعال تعال تعال

GEL, GEL, GEL
VIENS, VIENS, VIENS
KOMM, KOMM, KOMM
VEN, VEN, VEN
VEM, VEM, VEM
VIENI, VIENI, VIENI
ELA, ELA, ELA
CHODZ, CHODZ, CHODZ
EJA, EJA, EJA
BOO, BOO, BOO
ПРИЙДИ, ПРИЙДИ, ПРИЙДИ

بیا بیا بیا

To understand the ultimate truth of *why we are here and now on this planet* and *what there is after this life*, we should address our own selves, not others, and listen to our logic, intellect and conscience while observing calmly the signals of our heart.

Our heart, as a centre of our essence-consciousness, knows all the answers. Through the geometry of God's love, which keeps everything together in a thriving whole and maps out a perfect reflection/communication path, our heart is connected to the atoms of all our cells — the same way as it is connected to stars, universes and the eternal oneness.

MEMENTO 1

Learning to align with the Flow cannot be done with the mind alone. It is a choice that is made at levels much deeper than the ego or mind. It is a choice where the ego or mind aligns with the Higher Aspect as it works with the Flow Of Divine Creative Intelligence.
The only way to find this path forward is to go within and listen to the Inner Voice of the Heart.

Archangel Michael
through Celia Fenn

Mevlana Celaleddin-i Rumi

...ug, I became an Animal, I became a Human Being and later I will become Light.

GOLDEN AGE

ENDNOTES

OUR ONLY TIME IS NOW

I-1 *The Knowledge Book*, given through Vedia Bülent (Önsü) Çorak, contains the frequencies of all sacred books, revealed to our planet so far, together with the frequency of the *Mighty Energy Focal Point*. It is a *Universal Constitution* of the *Lordly order* also called the *Golden Book of the Golden Age* or the *Book of Truth*. All references relate to hardcover book (Second Edition, January 1998); www.dkb-mevlana.org.tr

I-2 More about the evolution and energy dimensions of the solar systems in *The Knowledge Book* – Vedia Bülent (Önsü) Çorak, Fascicule 44, pages 739-744

I-3 *The Dimension of the All-Truthful* – part of the drawing taken from *The Knowledge Book* – Vedia Bülent (Önsü) Çorak, Fascicule 46, pages 779-782

I-4 Vedia Bülent (Önsü) Çorak *The Knowledge Book*, Fascicule 26, page 410

I-5 Kryon – Magnetic entity, channelled through Lee Carroll; www.kryon.com

I-6 Saint Germain, an ascended master from spiritual hierarchy who works with the purifying power of *Violet Ray;* www.saintgermainfoundation.org

I-7 Noel Huntley, PhD, English scientist with a background in physics and doctorates in psychology and parapsychology, also a talented painter and musician, with a keen interest in computers. He has developed the foundation for a spiritual science as well as for the physics of a higher dimensional consciousness. Some of his books are: *ET and ALIENS: Who Are They? And Why Are They Here?; The Scientific Principles of Spiritual Enslavement* and *Attainment of Superior Physical Abilities and the New Science of Body Motion.* His website *Beyond Duality* is a collection of articles on variety of topics, like evolution, the nature of time, ascension, consciousness, holographic civilisation, fractals, types of physics and the theory of one; www.users.globalnet.co.uk/~noelh

I-8 More about *thought* in *The Knowledge Book*, by Vedia Bülent (Önsü) Çorak, Fascicule 29, pages 453 -454 and on influence of *Technological dimension* on our thoughts in Fascicule 25, page 381, par 8-9

I-9 Sándor Kabai is a mechanical engineer specialising in aviation and manufacturing technology. He is a member of the Geometry and Space Research Team – an inter-disciplinary group hosted by the Academy of Sciences and various universities in Hungary. On his website complex mathematical graphics can be found; www.kabai.hu

I-10 *Memento* – a Latin word used with its Latin language meaning: *do remember, do not forget.*

I-11 Quotation from *The Quran*, hand written in Arabic by Hussein Selim.

I-12 Flo Aeveia Magdalena is an author, medium, healer and teacher who founded *Soul Support Systems* and the *Heaven On Earth Global Community;* www.soulsupportsystems.org

I-13 Daniel Winter, a writer and lecturer in the areas of electrical engineering, psychophysiology (the origin of languages), computer animation in multimedia and non-linear energy source technologies. Winter developed superior technology for measuring coherent emotions in the heart *(HeartTuner*, also called *BlissTuner).* In his research and practical work he bridges the physical with the metaphysical; www.fractalfield.com

I-14   *The Möbius strip* is named after the German astronomer and mathematician August Ferdinand Möbius (1790-1868) who devised it in September 1858. Independently, two months earlier, another German mathematician of Czech ancestry, Johann Benedict Listing (1808-1882), came up with the same concept.

I-15   Suzanne Ward, through mental telepathy, records messages from Matthew, her son from the world of Spirit. Her books *(Matthew Books)* brought about in this way are: *Matthew, tell me about Heaven; Revelations for a new era, Illumination for a new era* and *Voices of the Universe*; www.matthewbooks.com

I-16   Emily Elizabeth Dickinson (1830-1886) was a prolific American poet. She was known to have written at least 133,700 poems, but only a very small number were published during her lifetime – most likely without her knowledge or anonymously. Later on she became regarded as one of the greatest 19th century American poets.

ETERNAL CHANGING

II-1   Sheldan Nidle is a representative and lecturer for the *Galactic Federation of Light*. He founded the *Planetary Activation Organization (PAO)* in November 1997; www.paoweb.com

II-2   Vedia Bülent (Önsü) Çorak, *The Knowledge Book,* Fascicule 43, page 733

II-3   Vedia Bülent (Önsü) Çorak, speech on 27/10/2009, Istanbul

II-4   Vedia Bülent (Önsü) Çorak, *The Knowledge Book,* Fascicule 26, pages 407-412

II-5   Vedia Bülent (Önsü) Çorak, *The Knowledge Book,* Fascicule 9, pages 135-136

II-6   Vedia Bülent (Önsü) Çorak, *The Knowledge Book,* Supplement 6, pages 1072-1074

II-7   Vedia Bülent (Önsü) Çorak, *The Knowledge Book,* Supplement 5, page 1060

II-8   Vedia Bülent (Önsü) Çorak, *The Knowledge Book,* Fascicule 46, pages 772-776; 778-779 and 783-784

II-9   Vedia Bülent (Önsü) Çorak, *The Knowledge Book,* Supplement 5, pages 1052-1054

II-10   Vedia Bülent (Önsü) Çorak, *The Knowledge Book,* Supplement 5, pages 1054 and 1061

II-11   On Beta Nova: *The Knowledge Book,* Vedia Bülent (Önsü) Çorak, Fascicule 46, pages 770-771 and 783

II-12   *The Knowledge Book* energy field images, used for the background of this chapter, produced by SUPRA Research Foundation, India

II-13   More on the cipher of Mevlana, the slogan *Come-Come-Come,* in *The Knowledge Book,* Vedia Bülent (Önsü) Çorak, Fascicule 7, pages 108-110

Front cover: Detail of the *Dimension of the All-Truthful* (see I-3)
Graphic design of the book: zodrag@gmail.com

BIBLIOGRAPHY

- ANTI-GRAVITY & THE WORLD GRID, edited by David Hatcher Childress; Adventures Unlimited Press
- THE ANCIENT SECRETS OF THE FLOWER OF LIFE, Volume 1 & 2 by Drunvalo Melchizedek; Sedona Color Graphics
- A BEGINNER'S GUIDE TO CONSTRUCTING THE UNIVERSE – The mathematical archetypes of Nature, Art, and Science a voyage from 1 to 10 by Michael S. Schneider; Harper Perennial, a division of Harper Collins Publishers
- CELTIC SPIRALS – handbook by Sheila Sturrock; Guild of Master Craftsman Publication Ltd
- FENG SHUI – The Traditional Oriental Way to Enhance Your Life by Stephen Skinner; Siena book, an imprint of Parragon
- THE FRACTAL GEOMETRY OF NATURE by Benoit B. Mandelbrot; W. H. Freeman and Company, New York
- THE GEOMETRY OF ART AND LIFE by Matila Ghyka; Dover Publications, inc. New York
- HIDDEN NATURE – The Startling Insights of Viktor Schauberger by Alick Bartholomew; Floris Books
- THE IMPLOSIONS' GRAND ATTRACTOR – Sacred Geometry & Coherent Emotion; assembled, Edited & Distributed from Daniel Winter's writing by Implosion Group
- ISLAMIC PATTERNS – An Analytical and Cosmological Approach by Keith Critchlow; Thames and Hudson, London
- JUST SIX NUMBERS – The Deep Forces that Shape the Universe by Martin Rees; Weidenfeld & Nicolson – London
- THE KNOWLEDGE BOOK – Messages received and transformed into writing by Vedia Bülent (Önsü) Çorak; World Brotherhood Union Mevlana Supreme Foundation, Istanbul
- L' ASTROLOGIE SACRE – Miroir de la Grande Tradition, Frederic Lionel; Editions du Rocher, Monaco
- LET THE NUMBERS GUIDE YOU – The Spiritual Science of Numerology by Shiv Charan Singh; O Books, Winchester, UK; New York, USA
- MAGIC SYMBOLS by Frederick Goodman; Brian Trodd Publishing House Limited
- THE MASTER MASONS OF CHARTRES by John James; West Grinstead Publishing
- NATURE'S NUMBERS – Discovering Order And Pattern In The Universe by Ian Stewart; Weidenfeld & Nicolson – London
- NUMEROLOGY with Tantra, Ayurveda, and Astrology – A Key to Human Behaviour by Harish Johari; Destiny Books, Rochester, Vermont
- ORDER IN SPACE – A Design Source Book by Keith Critchlow; Thames and Hudson, London
- PATTERN AND DESIGN WITH DYNAMIC SYMMETRY – How to Create Art Deco Geometrical Design by Edward B. Edwards; Dover Publications, inc, New York
- RANDOMNESS by Deborah J. Bennett; Harvard University Press, Cambridge, Massachusetts, London England
- SACRED GEOMETRY by Miranda Lundy; Wooden Books Ltd
- SACRED GEOMETRY – Philosophy and practice by Robert Lawlor; Thames and Hudson
- SECRETS OF ANCIENT AND SACRED PLACES – The world's Mysterious Heritage by Paul Devereux; Brockhampton Press, London
- SUNLIGHT ON WATER – A Manual for Soul-full Living – The One With No Names through Flo Aeveia Magdalena
- SYMMETRY IN CHAOS – A Search for Pattern in mathematics, Art and Nature by Michael Field and Martin Golubitsky; Oxford University Press
- THE JOY OF PI by David Plather; Bath Press Colourbooks, Glasgow
- THE SECRET SCIENCE OF ECSTASY AND IMMORTALITY – IMPLOSION by Daniel Winter
- THE TRUE POWER OF WATER – Healing And Discovering Ourselves by Masaru Emoto; Beyond Words Publishing, Inc., Hillsboro, Oregon
- YANTRA – The Tantric Symbol of Cosmic Unity by Madhu Khanna; Thames and Hudson

Copyright © Milena 2015
All rights reserved.

No part of this publication may be reproduced,
stored in or introduced into a retrieval system, or
transmitted, in any form, or by any means (electronic,
mechanical, photocopying, recording, or otherwise)
without the prior written permission of the
copyright owner.

Published by
M PUBLISHING
www.memento13.com

A catalogue record for this book is available from
the British Library

ISBN
978-1-909323-00-1

www.ingramcontent.com/pod-product-compliance
Lightning Source LLC
Chambersburg PA
CBHW060808090426
42736CB00002B/205